To My Darling Melissa,

Happy Valentines Day,

Love,

Mommie

shakespeare on Love

shakespeare on

Love

**Andrews McMeel
Publishing**

Kansas City

For information, write
Andrews McMeel Publishing,
an Andrews McMeel Universal company,
4520 Main Street, Kansas City, Missouri 64111.

www.andrewsmcmeel.com

ISBN: 0-7407-0363-3

Library of Congress Catalog Card Number:
99-62890

Produced by Smallwood & Stewart, Inc.
New York City
Designed by Debra Sfetsios

Table of Contents

he man who bequeathed his wife "the second-best bed with the furniture" (and nothing else) might be construed as something less than an ardent lover. Yet William Shakespeare must have been profoundly well acquainted with love in all its glory and its grief to have created so many acute portraits of those in its thrall. His characters revel in love, obsess about it, rail against it, weep for it, even give up their lives for it. And, just like people in real life, they often pass from one of these emotional states to another in the space of a moment. The same Rosalind (in *As You Like It*) who mocks Orlando's declaration that he will die of love is in the next second proclaiming her own love to be as bottomless as the Bay of Portugal. Looking down on his beloved Desdemona (in *Othello, the Moor of Venice*) as she lies asleep, Othello ricochets from rage to adoration even as he plans her murder. Hamlet is by turns mocking, cynical, disgusted, and tender as he contemplates love—and lust.

Since most people have been similarly conflicted in the course of their own love lives, we thought it would be amusing to offer up a sampling of excerpts from Shakespeare that would give voice to love's many diverse moods. Beginning with extravagantly inconsistent general observations and advice and then proceeding, mood by mood, with words from Shakespeare's ever-variable lovers,

these passages mirror the full
range of contradictions experienced
by those of us who have loved
perhaps not wisely but too well.

Observations & Advice

AY ME! FOR AUGHT THAT
I COULD EVER READ,
COULD EVER HEAR BY TALE OR HISTORY,
THE COURSE OF TRUE LOVE
NEVER DID RUN SMOOTH.

A Midsummer-Night's Dream

ACT I, SCENE I

(LOVE IS) AS SWEET AND MUSICAL

AS BRIGHT APOLLO'S LUTE,

STRUNG WITH HIS HAIR;

AND WHEN LOVE SPEAKS,

THE VOICE OF ALL THE GODS

MAKE HEAVEN DROWSY

WITH THE HARMONY.

Love's Labour's Lost

ACT IV, SCENE III

❧ 15 ❧

LOVE IS FULL OF UNBEFITTING STRAINS,

ALL WANTON AS A CHILD, SKIPPING,

AND VAIN.

Love's Labour's Lost

ACT V, SCENE II

BASE MEN BEING IN LOVE

HAVE THEN A NOBILITY

IN THEIR NATURES MORE THAN IS NATIVE

TO THEM.

Othello, the Moor of Venice

O, BEWARE, MY LORD, OF JEALOUSY!

IT IS THE GREEN-EY'D MONSTER WHICH

DOTH MOCK

THE MEAT IT FEEDS ON.

Othello, the Moor of Venice

ACT III, SCENE III

LOVE IS A SPIRIT ALL COMPACT OF FIRE,

NOT GROSS TO SINK, BUT LIGHT, AND

WILL ASPIRE.

Venus and Adonis

BUT EARTHLIER HAPPY
IS THE ROSE DISTILL'D
THAN THAT WHICH WITHERING ON THE
VIRGIN THORN
GROWS, LIVES, AND DIES IN SINGLE
BLESSEDNESS.

A Midsummer-Night's Dream

ACT I, SCENE I

HOT BLOOD BEGETS HOT THOUGHTS,

AND HOT THOUGHTS BEGET

HOT DEEDS,

AND HOT DEEDS IS LOVE.

Troilus and Cressida

ACT III, SCENE I

LOVE LOOKS NOT WITH THE EYES
BUT WITH THE MIND,
AND THEREFORE IS WING'D CUPID
PAINTED BLIND.

A Midsummer-Night's Dream

ACT I, SCENE I

The Ardent Lover

O, SHE DOTH TEACH THE TORCHES

TO BURN BRIGHT!

IT SEEMS SHE HANGS UPON THE CHEEK

OF NIGHT

AS A RICH JEWEL IN AN ETHIOP'S EAR;

BEAUTY TOO RICH FOR USE,

FOR EARTH TOO DEAR!

SO SHOWS A SNOWY DOVE TROOPING

WITH CROWS,

AS YONDER LADY O'ER HER

FELLOWS SHOWS.

THE MEASURE DONE,
I'LL WATCH HER PLACE OF STAND,
AND, TOUCHING HERS, MAKE BLESSED
MY RUDE HAND.
DID MY HEART LOVE TILL NOW?
FORSWEAR IT, SIGHT!
FOR I NE'ER SAW TRUE BEAUTY TILL THIS
NIGHT.

Romeo and Juliet

ACT I, SCENE V
(ROMEO UPON FIRST SIGHT OF JULIET)

WHO EVER LOV'D THAT LOV'D NOT AT

FIRST SIGHT?

As You Like It

ACT III, SCENE V
(THE SHEPHERDESS PHEBE, QUOTING A LINE
FROM CHRISTOPHER MARLOWE)

COME, GENTLE NIGHT, COME, LOVING,

BLACK-BROW'D NIGHT,

GIVE ME MY ROMEO; AND,

WHEN [HE] SHALL DIE,

TAKE HIM AND CUT HIM OUT IN LITTLE STARS,

AND HE WILL MAKE THE FACE OF

HEAVEN SO FINE

AND ALL THE WORLD WILL BE IN LOVE

WITH NIGHT

AND PAY NO WORSHIP TO THE GARISH SUN.

Romeo and Juliet

ACT III, SCENE II

❧ *30* ❧

I AM GIDDY; EXPECTATION WHIRLS

ME ROUND.

Troilus and Cressida

ACT III, SCENE II

(TROILUS AWAITING HIS BELOVED)

GOOD-NIGHT, GOOD-NIGHT! PARTING IS

SUCH SWEET SORROW,

THAT I SHALL SAY GOOD-NIGHT

TILL IT BE MORROW.

Romeo and Juliet

ACT II, SCENE II
(JULIET AFTER HER FIRST ENCOUNTER WITH ROMEO)

DOUBT THOU THE STARS ARE FIRE,

DOUBT THAT THE SUN DOTH MOVE,

DOUBT TRUTH TO BE A LIAR,

BUT NEVER DOUBT I LOVE.

Hamlet, Prince of Denmark

ACT II, SCENE II
(HAMLET'S DISINGENUOUS NOTE TO OPHELIA—
THOUGH HE DID INDEED LOVE HER)

THAT THOU DIDST KNOW HOW MANY
FATHOM DEEP I AM IN LOVE!
BUT IT CANNOT BE SOUNDED.
MY AFFECTION HATH AN UNKNOWN
BOTTOM, LIKE THE BAY OF PORTUGAL.

As You Like It

ACT IV, SCENE I
(ROSALIND ON HER LOVE FOR ORLANDO)

SHALL I COMPARE THEE TO A
SUMMER'S DAY?
THOU ART MORE LOVELY AND
MORE TEMPERATE:
ROUGH WINDS DO SHAKE THE DARLING
BUDS OF MAY,
AND SUMMER'S LEASE HATH ALL TOO
SHORT A DATE.

Sonnet 18

The Lover as Realist

My story being done,
She gave me for my pains a world
Of [sighs].
She swore, in faith, 'twas strange,
'Twas passing strange,
'Twas pitiful,
'Twas wondrous pitiful.
She wish'd she had not heard it;
Yet she wish'd
That Heaven had made her
Such a man.
She thank'd me,
And bade me, if I had a friend

✧ 38 ✧

THAT LOV'D HER,

I SHOULD BUT TEACH HIM HOW

TO TELL MY STORY,

AND THAT WOULD WOO HER.

UPON THIS HINT I SPAKE:

SHE LOV'D ME FOR THE DANGERS

I HAD PASS'D,

AND I LOV'D HER THAT

SHE DID PITY THEM.

Othello, the Moor of Venice

ACT I, SCENE III
(OTHELLO DESCRIBING HIS COURTSHIP OF DESDEMONA)

Song

WHO IS SILVIA? WHAT IS SHE,

THAT ALL OUR SWAINS COMMEND HER?

HOLY, FAIR, AND WISE IS SHE;

THE HEAVEN SUCH GRACE DID

LEND HER,

THAT SHE MIGHT ADMIRED BE.

IS SHE KIND AS SHE IS FAIR?

FOR BEAUTY LIVES WITH KINDNESS.

LOVE DOTH TO HER EYES REPAIR

To help him of his blindness,
And, being help'd, inhabits there.

Then to Silvia let us sing
That Silvia is excelling;
She excels each mortal thing
Upon the dull earth dwelling.
To her let us garlands bring.

The Two Gentlemen of Verona

ACT IV, SCENE II

MY MISTRESS' EYES ARE NOTHING
LIKE THE SUN;
CORAL IS FAR MORE RED
THAN HER LIPS' RED;
IF SNOW BE WHITE,
WHY THEN HER BREASTS ARE DUN;
IF HAIRS BE WIRES,
BLACK WIRES GROW ON HER HEAD.
I HAVE SEEN ROSES DAMASK'D, RED AND WHITE,
BUT NO SUCH ROSES SEE I
IN HER CHEEKS;
AND IN SOME PERFUMES IS
THERE MORE DELIGHT

THAN IN THE BREATH THAT

FROM MY MISTRESS REEKS.

I LOVE TO HEAR HER SPEAK, YET WELL I KNOW

THAT MUSIC HATH A FAR MORE

PLEASING SOUND;

I GRANT I NEVER SAW A GODDESS GO;

MY MISTRESS, WHEN SHE WALKS,

TREADS ON THE GROUND:

AND YET, BY HEAVEN,

I THINK MY LOVE AS RARE

AS ANY SHE BELI'D WITH FALSE

COMPARE.

Sonnet 130

Rosalind:

NOW TELL ME HOW LONG YOU

WOULD HAVE HER

AFTER YOU HAVE POSSESS'D HER.

Orlando:

FOR EVER AND A DAY.

Rosalind:

SAY "A DAY," WITHOUT THE

"EVER." NO, NO, ORLANDO.

MEN ARE APRIL WHEN THEY WOO,

DECEMBER WHEN THEY WED;

MAIDS ARE MAY WHEN THEY ARE MAIDS,

BUT THE SKY CHANGES WHEN

THEY ARE WIVES.

As You Like It

ACT IV, SCENE I

Song

Tell me where is fancy bred,

Or in the heart or in the head?

How begot, how nourished?

Reply, reply.

It is engend'red in the eyes,

With gazing fed; and fancy dies

In the cradle where it lies.

Let us all ring fancy's knell;

I'll begin it, —Ding, dong, bell.

The Merchant of Venice
ACT III, SCENE II

Song

WHAT IS LOVE? 'TIS NOT HEREAFTER.

PRESENT MIRTH HATH PRESENT LAUGHTER;

WHAT'S TO COME IS STILL UNSURE.

IN DELAY THERE LIES NO PLENTY;

THEN COME KISS ME, SWEET AND TWENTY,

YOUTH'S A STUFF WILL NOT ENDURE.

Twelfth Night; or, What You Will

ACT II, SCENE III

Song

Sigh no more, ladies, sigh no more,

Men were deceivers ever,

One foot in sea and one on shore,

To one thing constant never.

Then sigh not so, but let them go,

And be you blithe and bonny,

Converting all your sounds of woe

Into Hey nonny nonny.

Much Ado About Nothing

ACT II, SCENE I

The Lunatic Lover

Love is merely a madness, and,

I tell you,

Deserves as well a dark house

And a whip as madmen do;

And the reason why

They are not so punish'd and cured is,

That the lunacy

Is so ordinary

That the whippers

Are in love too.

As You Like It

Act III, Scene II

MEN HAVE DIED

FROM TIME TO TIME

AND WORMS HAVE EATEN THEM,

BUT NOT FOR LOVE.

As You Like It

ACT IV, SCENE I

(ROSALIND TO ORLANDO, WHEN HE DECLARES HE WILL DIE
IF HE CANNOT HAVE HIS BELOVED)

LOVERS AND MADMEN HAVE SUCH

SEETHING BRAINS,

SUCH SHAPING FANTASIES,

THAT APPREHEND MORE THAN COOL

REASON EVER COMPREHENDS.

THE LUNATIC, THE LOVER,

AND THE POET

ARE OF IMAGINATION ALL COMPACT.

A Midsummer-Night's Dream

ACT V, SCENE I

LORD, WHAT FOOLS THESE MORTALS BE!

A Midsummer-Night's Dream

ACT III, SCENE II

(PUCK DESCRIBING THE BEHAVIOR OF THE MOON-MAD LOVERS
IN THE FOREST)

REASON AND LOVE KEEP LITTLE
COMPANY TOGETHER NOW-A-DAYS.

A Midsummer-Night's Dream

ACT III, SCENE I
(BOTTOM TO TITANIA, WHO,
UNDER THE NEFARIOUS INFLUENCE OF A SPELL, HAS JUST
DECLARED HER QUITE UNREASONABLE LOVE FOR HIM)

WE THAT ARE TRUE LOVERS RUN INTO

STRANGE CAPERS.

As You Like It

ACT II, SCENE IV

IF EVER THOU SHALT LOVE,

IN THE SWEET PANGS OF IT REMEMBER ME;

FOR SUCH AS I AM ALL TRUE LOVERS ARE,

UNSTAID AND SKITTISH IN ALL

MOTIONS ELSE,

SAVE IN THE CONSTANT IMAGE

OF THE CREATURE

THAT IS BELOV'D.

Twelfth Night; or, What You Will

ACT II, SCENE IV

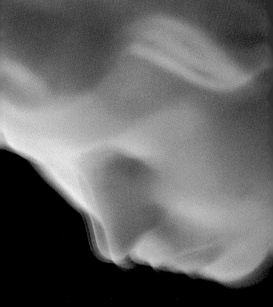

The
Melancholy
Lover

Song

TAKE, O TAKE THOSE LIPS AWAY,

THAT SO SWEETLY WERE FORSWORN;

AND THOSE EYES, THE BREAK OF DAY,

LIGHTS THAT DO MISLEAD THE MORN;

BUT MY KISSES BRING AGAIN,

BRING AGAIN;

SEALS OF LOVE, BUT SEAL'D IN VAIN,

SEAL'D IN VAIN.

Measure for Measure

ACT IV, SCENE I

If music be the food of love,

Play on!

Give me excess of it, that, surfeiting,

The appetite may sicken,

And so die.

Twelfth Night; or, What You Will

Act I, Scene I

The Doomed Lover

Then must you speak

Of one that lov'd not wisely

But too well.

Othello, the Moor of Venice

Act V, Scene II
(Othello, after realizing he has wrongly
slain Desdemona)

The crown o' th' earth doth melt.
My lord!
O, wither'd is the garland of the war,
The soldier's pole is fall'n!
Young boys and girls
Are level now with men;
The odds is gone,
And there's nothing left
Remarkable
Beneath the visiting moon.

Antony and Cleopatra

Act IV, Scene XV
(Cleopatra at Antony's death)

EYES, LOOK YOUR LAST!

ARMS, TAKE YOUR LAST EMBRACE!

AND, LIPS, O YOU THE DOORS OF
BREATH,

SEAL WITH A RIGHTEOUS KISS

A DATELESS BARGAIN TO ENGROSSING DEATH!

. . . HERE'S TO MY LOVE!

[DRINKS] O TRUE APOTHECARY!

THY DRUGS ARE QUICK. THUS WITH A
KISS I DIE.

Romeo and Juliet

ACT V, SCENE III
(ROMEO, KILLING HIMSELF, IN THE BELIEF THAT JULIET IS DEAD)

FOR NEVER WAS A STORY OF MORE WOE
THAN THIS OF JULIET AND HER ROMEO.

Romeo and Juliet

ACT V, SCENE III

The
Disillusioned
Lover

FRAILTY, THY NAME IS WOMAN!

Hamlet, Prince of Denmark

ACT I, SCENE II, 146

O CURSE OF MARRIAGE,

THAT WE CAN CALL THESE DELICATE

CREATURES OURS,

AND NOT THEIR APPETITES!

Othello, the Moor of Venice

ACT III, SCENE III

Ophelia:

'TIS BRIEF, MY LORD.

Hamlet:

AS WOMAN'S LOVE.

Hamlet, Prince of Denmark

ACT III, SCENE II

FOR I HAVE SWORN THEE FAIR, AND

THOUGHT THEE BRIGHT,

WHO ART AS BLACK AS HELL,

AS DARK AS NIGHT.

Sonnet 147

LECHERY, LECHERY;

STILL WARS AND LECHERY;

NOTHING ELSE HOLDS FASHION.

Troilus and Cressida

ACT V, SCENE II
(THERSITES, AFTER WATCHING CRESSIDA BETRAY TROILUS)

THERE LIVES WITHIN THE VERY FLAME

OF LOVE

A KIND OF WICK OR SNUFF THAT WILL

ABATE IT.

Hamlet, Prince of Denmark

ACT IV, SCENE VII
(KING CLAUDIUS, SEDUCER OF THE WOMAN WHOSE
HUSBAND HE MURDERED, THUS SOMETHING OF AN EXPERT
ON LOVE'S TRANSIENCE)

True Love

LET ME NOT TO THE MARRIAGE OF
TRUE MINDS
ADMIT IMPEDIMENTS. LOVE IS NOT LOVE
WHICH ALTERS WHEN IT
ALTERATION FINDS,
OR BENDS WITH THE REMOVER
TO REMOVE.
O, NO! IT IS AN EVER-FIXED MARK
THAT LOOKS ON TEMPESTS AND IS
NEVER SHAKEN; IT IS THE STAR TO EVERY
WAND'RING BARK,
WHOSE WORTH'S UNKNOWN,
ALTHOUGH HIS HEIGHT BE TAKEN.

Love's not Time's fool, though rosy
Lips and cheeks
Within his bending sickle's
Compass come;
Love alters not with his brief hours
And weeks,
But bears it out even to the
Edge of doom.
If this be error and
Upon me proved,
I never writ, nor no man
Ever loved.

Sonnet 116

Photo Credits